A GUIDE TO UNDERSTANDING THE
CRIMINAL JUSTICE SYSTEM: SEX CRIMES

DARRYL A. STALLWORTH, ESQ.
Attorney at Law

DARRYL A. STALLWORTH
LAW OFFICE

Jacobs & Whitehall
73-03 Bell Blvd, #10
Oakland Gardens, NY 11364
www.jacobsandwhitehall.com
(888) 570-7338

Ordering Information:

Quantity sales. Special discounts are available on quantity purchases by corporations, associations, and others. For details, contact the publisher at the address above.

Orders by U.S. trade bookstores and wholesalers. Please contact Jacobs & Whitehall at Tel: (888) 570-7338 or visit www.jacobsandwhitehall.com.

Printed in the United States of America

Published in 2020

ISBN: 978-1-951149-39-0

PREFACE

Nothing prepares you for life better than experience. The same can be said of understanding the law. You can study life but not truly understand it unless you have lived for a while. I studied law for three years. I have taken and passed two State Bar exams. I've read numerous cases, statutes and laws. My true education, however, did not start until the first day a walked into a courtroom in November of 1992 and argued my first case. I learned the application of the law is vastly different than the study of the law. Similar to the journey of life one must "live" the law in order to truly understand it. I've been living the "law" for 29 years, 15 years as a prosecutor and the past 14 years as a criminal defense attorney. The experience has provided me with a very unique understanding of the Criminal Justice System. This book and those to follow will provide a better understanding of a system that can tragically impact your life.

DEDICATION

I was born on January 16, 1965; 102 years after President Lincoln issued the Emancipation Proclamation on January 1, 1863. However, freedom for my ancestors would only come when the Union Army defeated the Confederate Army. Indeed the 1863 Emancipation Proclamation gave African Americans the right to fight in the war. Nonetheless, it took another two years, specifically not until April 1865 before the Confederate Army surrendered and my ancestors, in theory became free.

In writing this book I stand on the shoulders of my ancestors and other heroes who physically fought for a freedom that they ultimately came to know would not be truly realized for years to come.

I dedicate this book to everyone who sacrificed their lives so that men and women of all races would have an opportunity to live a purposeful life.

ACKNOWLEDGMENTS

Writing a book has been on my list of things to do for so long, but I was not sure if it would ever happen. As with everything in life, it required patience, discipline, and considerable support. I want to thank my family and friends who encouraged and inspired me to write this book. I want to also thank those of you who provided your input and took time to read and edit my numerous drafts.

DISCLAIMER

This publication is intended to be used for educational purposes only. No legal advice is being given, and no attorney-client relationship is intended to be created by reading this material. The author assumes no liability for any errors or omissions or for how this book or its contents are used or interpreted or for any consequences resulting directly or indirectly from the use of this book. For legal or any other advice, please consult an experienced attorney or the appropriate expert who is aware of the specific facts of your case and is knowledgeable of the law in your jurisdiction.

Darryl A. Stallworth Law Office
2355 Broadway
Suite 303
Oakland, CA
www.your-defense.com
(510) 917-5270

TESTIMONIALS

"This attorney came as a result of a dear friend of mine. A close family member was facing the death penalty. Upon speaking with Mr. Stallworth his calm and humble nature were enough to select him. He just made us feel like he cared about us, and understood the emotions we were encountering. Over a 4.5 year period, there were periodic meetings between Mr. Stallworth and his client who remained in jail while awaiting trial. Although the drive to see his client took several hours he never complained. When the time for trial finally arrived, Mr. Stallworth armored with his strong faith intact, having done homework from every possible angle, went to task. After a three month trial, my family could not be more pleased with the outcome... Charges were DISMISSED and our family member is FREE!!

I highly recommend this attorney. He's a fighter for his clients, and he's highly dedicated, competent, and he knows and understands the law. If you need an EXCELLENT lawyer, look no further."

Table Of Contents

ABOUT THE AUTHOR

Darryl Stallworth is from Compton, California and has resided in the Bay Area for over 35 years. As a teenager in the 1980s, Darryl watched his safe and caring community transform into one heavily impacted by gang violence and drug activity. He credits the support of his family, educators, coaches and his faith for keeping him focused on school and sports.

A scholar-athlete, Darryl excelled in football, baseball, soccer and track where he developed into a natural leader often serving as team captain. Those leadership skills were not just manifested in the sports' fields. They were also present in the classroom where Darryl served as Student Body President and class Valedictorian.

Darryl was awarded an academic scholarship to the University of California at Berkeley and arrived on campus in the fall of 1983. An earnest student, Darryl also had dreams of playing college football for the Golden Bears. He dedicated his mind to his studies and conditioned himself with hopes of making the team. Within two years, Darryl's dream was realized with a spot on the team and a full, athletic scholarship.

Darryl graduated with a degree in Political Science from Berkeley in 1987. He then turned his sights to law school at the University of California at Davis. It was during that time that he fell in love with trial work.

In 1992, Darryl started his legal career with the Alameda County District Attorney's Office. During the course of 15 years he conducted over 50 criminal trials, served as the Plea-Bargaining Deputy, and lectured in Brazil, Malaysia, India and Turkey on effective case resolutions.

In 2007 Darryl left the DA's office and became a partner with *Taylor, Goins and Stallworth.* In 2009 he started his firm, *The Law Office of Darryl A. Stallworth.*

"Over the past 14 years, I've dedicated my career to serving clients through the most challenging times of their lives while doing everything I can in the community to help others avoid this path. I've written this book to help anyone going through this complicated legal system and to serve as an educational tool for prevention."

INTRODUCTION

Although the criminal justice system is complex, wherever possible, this book is written using common terms. You don't have to be an attorney to understand this book's content. And, it's worth saying that while you don't have to be a lawyer to read this book, if you find yourself charged with a sex crime, you should find legal counsel as soon as possible.

The Stakes Are High

Jail is a funky place. It's crowded, it smells and is full of despair. Prison is worse. You've seen the movies. Yeah, it's pretty much like what you have seen. No matter how many nights and weekends I've spent visiting clients in jail, I'm always keenly aware of the palpable tension in the visiting room that manifests itself in that smell – it's the body's chemical reaction to the stress, sadness, and fear rising from the crowded, communal spaces. As bad as it smells, all things considered, when incarcerated, it will be the least of your concerns if you should ever find yourself in that unfortunate situation.

I cannot stress enough that jail is not a place you want to be. It's not a place where you want your parents, sisters, brothers, wife, husband, or kids visiting you. A sex crime conviction can put you there, and depending on the charges and your legal defense, take away your freedom.

Even with lesser incarceration, the impact of a sex crime conviction will have far-reaching consequences after release. Other than murder, there isn't a more defamatory charge. For example, you will be branded as a **sexual predator**. Imagine not being free to attend your child's school functions, being restricted from parks and playgrounds, and/or being around children (including your own) period. In many cases, you may be required to register as a sex offender which will dictate not only your freedom of movement, but ultimately your job/profession, and where you are allowed to live.

The stakes are high when it comes to sex crimes in California. Without basic knowledge or a guide to help you navigate the legal system, your actions could jeopardize your freedom. Now more than ever it's important to know your rights, and even more importantly, to know how to avoid situations where you can be accused of a sex crime.

CHAPTER 1

SEX CRIMES IN CALIFORNIA

In 2019 California had the second highest number of sex crimes in the United States with 14,799 reported cases. Texas was first with 14, 824 reported cases (Statista Research Department, September 2020).

The mere mention of a person being investigated for a sex crime usually conjures up images of the "dirty old man in a trench coat." This image however is outdated. Those accused of sex crimes are represented in all social and economic demographics and include men and women, the young and old, and from every walk of life and profession (athletes, doctors, clergy/church leaders, teachers, students, coaches, trade workers, etc.).

There are numerous categories of sex crimes in California. Depending on the facts the charges can be classified into two main categories: **misdemeanor** or **felony**.

Let's start by describing the legal criteria of a misdemeanor and then take a deeper dive into each category and examine the possible penalties. I've included real case examples and personal insights from my almost 30 years of working in this field. In these circumstances, the names of the parties involved have been changed to protect privacy.

Before reading further, it is important to note that the content going forward can be graphic and disturbing. Whenever possible, clinical terms are used to describe physical anatomy. While the subject matter can be distressing, it is critical to understand the legal specifics of each classification along with their respective penalty.

Misdemeanor Sex Crime

Definition: Non-consensual touching of the breasts, vaginal or male genital area, and/or the anus.

If Convicted:

- Possible incarceration in jail for up to a year

- May be required to complete three years of misdemeanor probation
- May be required to complete sex offender class
- May be required to register as a sex offender

Statutory Rape

In California, anyone who is 18 or over and has consensual sex with someone who is under the age of 18 could be charged with statutory rape. An 18-year-old having sex with a 17-year-old is rarely prosecuted; however, when it is, it is a misdemeanor that does not require sex offender registration.

If you're 21 or older and have consensual sex with someone under the age of 18, you could be charged with felony statutory rape. Oftentimes, it is the minor's parents who are reporting the crime. Felony statutory rapes could result in prison time and registration as a sex offender.

Felony Sex Crime

Definition: Non-consensual penetration of an object, finger, and/or penis into the vagina and/or anus.

- Vaginal penetration is considered rape
- Penetration of the anus is sodomy or rape
- Oral copulation is the non-consensual insertion of a penis into someone's mouth

If Convicted:

- Incarceration in prison, possibly for Life
- Register as a sex offender for life

Statute of Limitations

Penal Code Section 801.1 states that if you're under the age of 18 when the sex crime occurred you have up until your 40th birthday to request prosecution of the accused. If you're over 18 at the time of the sex crime you have 10 years to request prosecution of the accused.

Elements of a Case

The traditional elements that a prosecutor must prove in a sex crime are "force or fear". For example, the accuser was physically restrained or threatened with harm if they resisted. The less traditional, but more common element that a prosecutor must prove is exploitation. For example, the accuser suffers from an obvious mental impairment or is too intoxicated to provide consent.

It is this latter area of law that presents the most difficult challenges for the accused. Whether the accuser has a mental impairment or is intoxicated, it is likely they will be unable to remember in detail what happened. However, the accused is required by law to understand and appreciate whether or not the accuser had a mental impairment or was too intoxicated to consent.

Standard of Proof

"Beyond a reasonable doubt" is the standard of proof in a criminal case. But what exactly does that mean? I advise juries that "beyond a reasonable doubt" means a strong, enduring conviction that the person accused is responsible for the crime. If there is any doubt, and those doubts are reasonable, you cannot convict. The Defense is not required to prove that a person is innocent. It is entirely the burden of the Prosecution to prove guilt. **A case not proved demands a not-guilty verdict.**

While the standard of proof at trial requires a jury of 12 people to convict, charging someone with a sex crime is in the hands of the District Attorney's office.

When I was a young Prosecutor, I was taught that charging someone with a crime should not occur unless I could foresee that 12 people would consider the case and believe, beyond a reasonable doubt, that a person was responsible. Consequently, it may take a considerable amount of time before the Prosecutor files charges. Although this may cause considerable anxiety to the person accused, it is always better for the Prosecutor to take their time to carefully review the accusation before charging the case particularly when there is so much at stake.

A wrong decision charging decision in a sex crime can cause irreversible damage. Even if charges are later dismissed, the accused will endure a level of suspicion created by the arrest and charges alone.

Life Changing Impacts

Receiving a phone call or a knock at your door informing you that you're under investigation for a sex crime will undoubtedly be one of the scariest moments of your life. You will be presumed guilty until proven innocent in the court of public opinion.

In many circumstances, your job/profession is the first to be impacted with a suspension or administrative leave. The standard of review for a human resources department is quite different from the standard of review for the District Attorney's Office. Mere suspicion may be sufficient cause to furlough or dismiss an employee. If the accused is under investigation and continues to work, it puts the employer at risk of liability should a similar circumstance arise during their employment. Sadly, I've observed these scenarios many times where even the most respected employee with multiple years of service is terminated before the investigation is completed.

The cloud of suspicion not only impacts the livelihood of the accused but permeates all aspects of life. Some of the most hurtful circumstances arise from social shunning. Friends and family members pause to consider if the accused behaved in a certain way around their spouse, children, and friends. Invitations to dinner, family gatherings, and events evaporate and the accused begins to be treated as an outsider. They are unfortunately and unfairly presumed guilty.

How Does the Public Know?

As the adage goes, news travels fast and bad news travels faster. Add social media to the mix and bad news travels at light speed. Few headlines are more captivating than the news that someone has been charged with a sex crime. The media makes money from interesting and salacious stories. If you're a public figure, educator, coach, your story will get top billing and will be broadcasted over and over again.

A while back, I represented a college football coach. When the news broke that he was under investigation for a sex crime, the story was not only picked-up by every local station, but went viral on social media and ESPN. He was unable to go anywhere without being recognized or harassed by the media resulting in a traumatic, isolating situation.

In a similar circumstance, another client was accused of a sex crime and within hours his photo was featured on the news. Although I was able to resolve both cases and later have them dismissed, the damage had already been done.

CHAPTER 2

INVESTIGATION

Am I Under Investigation?

If you are under investigation for a sex crime, it is quite likely you'll be the last to know. The majority of people will not know they are being investigated until the investigation is nearing completion. Contacting you for the police interview is typically the last step.

You will notice a reoccurring theme throughout this book…retain the services of an attorney as soon as possible to assure the best defense possible.

Investigative Interview

If the police show up to ask you questions, do not feel obligated to speak with them. You have the right to remain silent. If they are going to arrest you they will do so whether you make a statement or not. Do not help them by giving a statement that can easily be misinterpreted. Under the stressful situation and at the hands of a skilled interviewer your statements could be perceived as deceptive or false.

It is important for you to remain calm, refrain from answering questions, and ask for an attorney.

If I Ask For An Attorney – Do I Look Guilty?

Requesting an attorney during an investigation does not make you look guilty, it makes you look smart. It is the most important thing you can do. When you hire an attorney, the police are aware that you understand the gravity of the situation and are taking a proactive approach to protect your constitutional rights and freedom. A phone call from an attorney puts the officer on notice that you have an advocate. In the Bay Area, I know many of the investigating officers from my prior work as a Prosecutor. There is mutual and professional respect which often results in a courtesy phone call before an arrest is made.

When I work with a client, my advocacy starts with a phone call to the investigatory agency. My next call is to the District Attorney's Office requesting a meeting or conversation with the charging prosecutor. Sometimes, I am able to provide the prosecutor with evidence from my own investigation in an effort to prevent my client from being charged. If I'm successful, it saves my client the trauma of an arrest and charge of a sex crime.

I'm Under Investigation - What Should I Do?

First and foremost, stay calm. It's likely that your head will be spinning. However, the quicker you can do the following actions, the easier you can navigate through the criminal justice system.

- **Retain an attorney or request one, immediately**

Be sure to find an attorney with expertise, knowledge, and trial experience with sex crimes.

- **Do NOT speak to anyone about the case – including your family**

It will be difficult, but it's important that you only speak to your attorney about your case to avoid miscommunication, misinterpretation, and/or inconsistencies.

I advise all of my clients that they are only allowed to speak with me about their case. In such a high stress situation, it's natural to want to talk to friends/family about events in question and/or the accuser, but it's critical to only discuss the case with your attorney.

- **Suspend ALL social media accounts**

Anything that you've posted on social media could be used as evidence against you. Have you ever posted an off-color joke, a racy picture of yourself, or someone of the opposite sex that could be interpreted negatively? Even something as innocent as a picture of your kids, niece, nephew, a kid's soccer game, or school play can be reframed out-of-context against you. Further, social media is not the forum to state your side of events or emote how upset you are about the charges.

Avoid the temptation - don't look at it, don't comment on any threads, just shut it down.

Mistakes to Avoid During an Investigation

- **DON'T speak to the Police**

Your only statement to the police should be **"Lawyer!"**

The most damaging mistake you can make is talking to the police. I know this seems counterintuitive, but this is the time to stay silent. When the police call you or show up at your door, it's natural to want to explain yourself to give your account of events. The officer(s) know that you're scared and nervous and likely to say something to defend yourself. They're counting on it. Often, they will find a way to make you feel comfortable and lull you into saying something that may incriminate you.

If you're being questioned about an event and you don't know what the other person knows about the event, you should not attempt to describe it to them.

Bottom line; don't talk to anyone about anything, particularly when they have more knowledge about the case than you do. Remember, the police have already spoken to witnesses, looked at videos, and/or completed a DNA analysis, before questioning you. Anything you say, even if it's true, can be perceived as deceptive. An innocent inaccurate recollection can be construed as untruthful.

- **DON'T contact or answer phone calls from the accuser**

Do not attempt to contact the accuser. Period. Nothing positive can come from direct confrontation with your accuser. Further, you could be additionally accused of harassment.

Never accept a phone call from the accuser. This call is very likely to be a "pretext call". This is where the accuser, with the coaching of a police officer, calls you to solicit an admission.

Accuser: "You know what you did was wrong. Why did you do that to me? You knew I was drunk/passed-out…."

You: "Yeah – I'm sorry about that."

Translation: you just made an admission of guilt. This will most certainly be used against you in any proceedings going forward.

Unfortunately, in many circumstances, the accused thinks they are helping an emotionally distraught accuser with a generally comforting statement; when in reality, they are making a statement that could be interpreted as an admission.

- **DON'T post anything on social media**

Avoid social media altogether. That means no posting, commenting, or conversing with friends. If you think that it's private, it's not. All of your information can be retrieved by the police. I've seen officers assume a false social media profile, gain access to your social media and start a conversation. This makes it extremely challenging to retroactively defend any statements, photos, or videos posted to your social media.

To put it plainly, you shouldn't make it easy for someone to investigate you. Taking a few proactive steps can help.

What's The Deal with DNA?

DNA plays a vital role in today's investigation. Most investigations are not complete until the DNA results are completed. A matching DNA result can confirm that the accused was at the scene and or had contact with the accuser.

A DNA match does not secure a guilty verdict. DNA evidence can only answer the "who" question. It does not answer the "what, when, where, and why" questions. A sex crime investigation often starts with a physical exam by the Sexual Assault Response Team (SART). This team will interview the accuser and conduct a head-to-toe physical examination that includes a thorough assessment of genitalia. The presence of the accused's DNA is just one of many factors to be considered in the case.

CHAPTER 3

ARREST

The Arrest Process

There are a number of ways you can be arrested. Someone can report to the police that you have committed a crime. The police arrive and if you are present you can be arrested on the spot. Most often a crime is reported, investigated and a warrant for your arrest is issued. Armed with an arrest warrant a police officer can arrest you on sight. Yes, that means you can be arrested at your job, your school, your home, or any social event you might be attending.

If you are represented by an attorney during the investigation process sometimes the police with assistance from your attorney will allow you to self-surrender. This is the ideal scenario but it rarely happens.

Most arrests follow a very basic protocol:

1. Transported to the local police department

2. Processed (Fingerprinted and logged in to criminal division data bank)
3. Mirandized (Read an admonition that informs you that you have the right to remain silent and the right to have a lawyer)
4. If you waive your right to remain silent and have an attorney you will then be questioned.
5. You are allowed a phone call but when you get to make that call varies.

If I'm Arrested - What Do I Need to Know?

In the stressful situation of arrest, there are three crucial items to remember…

1. **You have the right to remain silent**

Remaining silent means just that. Do not answer any questions. Investigators will do their best to get you talking. These individuals are pros and have conducted hundreds of interviews all design to get you to make a statement. Once you start answering questions, your defense becomes 100 times more challenging. Here's what you should do:

A. Remain calm

B. Put your head down

C. And say one word, "LAWYER".

2. You have the right to an attorney

Regardless of the charge, you have the right to an attorney. If you cannot afford one, an attorney will be provided. You do not need to have a private attorney to exercise your right to request one from the moment you are arrested.

3. You have the right to reasonable bail

Depending on the type of sex crime charge, bail may be set from fifty thousand to one million dollars. Most bail bond companies will charge you 10% of the bail and require collateral for the balance. If you are represented by an attorney they will sometimes only require 6-8% of the bail amount upfront.

CHAPTER 4

ACTIVE DEFENSE

Should I Represent Myself Or Use An Attorney?

Worst: You've read a few do's and don'ts so far and on the subject of self-representation for a sex crime, I'm sure you can guess which category this falls into. This is a huge DON'T. Representing yourself against a sex crime is the worst decision you can ever make. An attorney is necessary to ensure your rights, and ultimately, your freedom.

Better: If you cannot afford a private attorney, the Public Defender will assist you. Public Defenders often get a bad rap, but they are some of the best attorneys around. However, with the large caseloads that most Public Defenders carry, they can be less accessible than a private attorney. Additionally, when assigned a Public Defender, you do not have the ability to choose your attorney. It is possible to be assigned an attorney who is very talented, but lacks trial experience or an attorney that has a lot of trial experience, but is not very talented.

Best: Whenever possible, I highly recommend retaining the services of an experienced private attorney. Why? A good experienced private attorney will be more available to you. I know that my clients are in a highly stressful, traumatic time that doesn't regulate itself to a 9 to 5 schedule Monday through Friday. I've spent many late nights and weekends counseling clients throughout their case.

My Process: While I cannot speak about the methodology of all private attorneys, when I am retained by a new client, I often start by gathering as much case information as possible which can include:

- obtaining the police report
- speaking to the Prosecutor
- coordinating legal experts
- conducting my own investigation including a physical examination of the alleged crime scene
- researching the accuser's background

Real Case Results - Defense Investigation

A few years back, I had a client accused of sexual assault where the accuser claimed that she suffered from self-image issues as a result of the accused's conduct. She stated that she could no longer go outside and felt everyone was looking at her. Additionally, she was now uncomfortable around men and her relationships with men were destroyed.

An investigation into her background revealed social media images and video postings that suggested quite the opposite. Further, as part of the client's defense, we conducted a physical examination of the alleged crime scene where we obtained our own photo documentation, created maps, and the accuser's cell phone records were pulled. We also researched the accuser's background, history, prior reports, and psychiatric records.

The same thoroughness was applied to all potential witnesses, including police officers. As a result, we were able to discredit the foundation of the case and ultimately have the felony dismissed.

In another case, the investigation was vital to a proactive defense. A witness testified that the accuser was "an angel...didn't drink, and had never been in trouble before." My investigation uncovered a video of the witness and accuser consuming alcohol together. The witness lost all creditability with the jury. This case also resulted in a felony dismissal.

CHAPTER 5

PLEA BARGAINING

Plea Bargaining

Often referred to as a "deal," a plea bargain is any agreement in a criminal case between the prosecutors and accused whereby the accused agrees to plead guilty or no contest to a particular charge in return for some concession from the prosecutor. This may mean that the accused will plead guilty to a less serious charge or to one of several charges, in return for the dismissal of the other charges.

While a plea bargain is tempting in the face of a long uncertain trial, accepting a "deal" is not always best. An experienced and knowledgeable defense attorney is imperative to assist the accused with this decision.

Preliminary Hearing

Typically a plea offer will be made by the Prosecutor prior to the Preliminary Hearing. However, it can be beneficial to conduct the Preliminary Hearing before accepting an offer.

A preliminary hearing is commonly referred to as a "Probable Cause Hearing." It is a judicial hearing where the prosecutor is required to introduce enough evidence to convince the judge that it is likely the accused has committed the crime charged. This standard of review is vastly different than the reasonable doubt standard applied at trial. Most prosecutors only introduce the minimum amount of evidence required in order to prevail at a preliminary hearing. In cases involving a sex crime a prosecutor will almost always have the accuser testify.

The accused rarely introduces any evidence at a preliminary hearing. It is merely an opportunity to evaluate and challenge the credibility of the accuser.

I defended a case where five men were accused of kidnapping four young girls and subjecting them to various sex crimes. All four of the accusers testified during the preliminary hearing where I was able to challenge all of their conflicting and embellished descriptions of events.

After being caught in a web of lies the accusers refused to answer any more of my questions. At the end of the preliminary hearing, the five men were released from custody and offered plea deals that did not require incarceration or sex offender registration.

Plea offers can be **negotiated**. The facts of your case, the accuser's credibility, the strength of the witnesses, and the reputation of your legal representation can all affect your plea arrangement. In the negotiating process, it is not uncommon for offers to go back and forth a few times before ending up with an agreement that is acceptable to both sides.

When To Take A Plea Bargain Or Go To Trial?

Deciding to go to trial is a decision made with my client after I have completed my review of the case, conducted all of my investigation, and carefully weighed the likelihood of prevailing at trial. This decision is likely to be the most important decision my client has ever made. Consequently, it is imperative that I spend as much time as necessary meeting with my client and their family discussing every concern they may have. It is deeply concerning when I hear the decision to go to trial is made where an attorney has spent very little time reviewing the case with the client.

My clients have the benefit of knowing that I've carefully reviewed all the strengths and weaknesses of their case and that we have thoroughly discussed the decision to go to trial or accept a plea agreement. Oftentimes, we will discuss this decision for weeks, sometimes months, before a decision is made.

CHAPTER 6

THE TRIAL

Trial Preparation Is A Marathon Not A Sprint

Forget everything you've seen on TV where the investigation, arrest and trial are concluded in an hour episode. A trial is a process that requires a methodical approach. Many of my clients get anxious when the wheels of justice turn slowly. Moving slowly is often required to grind-out what we want or something close to it. My advice is to be patient with the process.

Pretrial Motions

Before a trial starts the prosecutor and the defense attorney will submit a motion requesting that the court make a decision on certain issues before the trial begins. The motions typically address jury selection, courtroom protocol, physical evidence and testimony.

Jury Selection

When a jury trial is ready to start, the court will request a panel of prospective jurors. The judge commonly begins the selection process by identifying those jurors who are unable to serve due to a legally recognized hardship. The judge and the lawyers then select the jury by a process known as "Voir Dire," which is Latin for "to speak the truth." In Voir Dire the judge and the attorneys ask potential jurors questions to determine if they can be a fair and impartial juror.

The Trial

The prosecutor has the burden of proof and thus is required to convince all 12 jurors that the accused is guilty beyond a reasonable doubt of the crime/crimes charged. The prosecutor will introduce the evidence through the testimony of officers, doctors, experts and the accused. The defense attorney challenges the prosecutor's evidence through cross examination. At the conclusion of the prosecutor's case the defense may but is not required to present a case. After both sides have rested the prosecutor delivers a closing argument followed by the defense attorney's closing argument which is then followed by the prosecutor's rebuttal argument. The judge will then read jury instructions to the jury. The jury can deliberate for as long as they like until they reach a verdict or conclude that they are unable to reach a unanimous decision resulting in a mistrial.

CHAPTER 7

CONVICTION & SENTENCING GUIDELINES

Conviction of a singular rape of one person (without any "enhancements") can carry a sentence of up to nine years in prison. Enhancements are additional allegations that can substantially increase the time spent in prison (for example use of weapons, serious injuries, violence). There are also underlying charges such as robbery or kidnapping that could result in a life sentence.

Do Penalties Differ From A Guilty Verdict Versus Taking A Deal?

The simple answer is, "yes". Receiving a more severe penalty than what the Prosecutor offered before trial is a major risk of going to trial. While no one will go on the record and state that they are going to punish you more severely because you challenged the Prosecutor's case by going to trial, it is often a reality.

For example, if the potential penalty for your charges is sixteen years in prison the Prosecutor may offer you four years before trial. If you are found guilty at trial, you will almost certainly be sentenced to 16 years.

Prison

At the beginning of this book, I remarked that jail is a funky place. As bad as jail is, prison is worse. Prison is a particularly dangerous place for sex offenders. There will be someone there that will want to hurt you. An inmate will try to brand you. This typically occurs with a sharp object to the face to create a scar (brand) notifying every one of the reason you are in prison.

CHAPTER 8

SEX OFFENDER REGISTRATION

The California Sex Offender Registry is designed to provide information to law enforcement and the general public about sex offenders. Most misdemeanor sex crimes do not require Sex Offender Registration. Felony cases almost always require registration.

Under Penal Code 290, California law requires that people convicted of certain crimes must register as a sex offender. A convicted sex offender must register with the local law enforcement agency annually within five days of his/her birthday and within five days upon moving residences. If you are in college you must register with the campus police. If your offense involved a minor you may not live near any school, or work for any place that comes into contact with kids or young adults. You will also have to notify your employer. In your county or city, there is a list that your name will appear on. Anyone who wants to find out about you can go to the list. It eliminates about 90% of the types of jobs you can get.

Recently, laws have been passed in California that have modified the lifetime requirement for registration as a sex offender. For example, sex crimes that are considered nonserious may only require a 10-year registration period.

Chapter 9

Innocence & Exoneration

If you were accused of a sex crime and ultimately not convicted, you will still have trouble getting work. I had a client who got exonerated but because of all the publicity of the case, it took a long time for people to overcome it. Although you've been exonerated or the case has been dismissed, most search engines will find a record showing that you've been arrested for a sex crime.

Just because you're arrested doesn't mean that you did it, particularly since you've been exonerated. However, if an employer has to choose between you and five other candidates who don't have an arrest for a sex crime it is unlikely that they are going to hire you.

How Someone Found Innocent or Exonerated In a Sex Crime Case Can Get Back To Normal Life

A person who has suffered an arrest that did not result in a conviction may petition the court to have their arrest and related records sealed. Getting a clean slate is the first step to your new life.

My advice would be to get the arrest expunged with my help and then find work that doesn't require an extensive background search. It won't be an easy journey but with the proper mindset it can be done.

CHAPTER 10

POLITICAL CLIMATE

Impact Of the "Me Too" Movement

The Tobin Center for Economic Policy conducted a research project which found that since the 2017 reporting of sex crimes by former movie producer Harvey Weinstein there has been a 13% increase in the reporting of sex crimes in the US. The "Me Too" movement has inspired many to share their experiences on social media or in the press. While this focus may be overdue, the movement has also shifted the way that many sex crime accusations are handled legally. The narrative has changed the presumption of innocence to the presumption of guilt and created a more receptive, sympathetic environment for accusers. Interestingly, while the numbers of reported sex crimes have increased, the numbers of sex crimes actually charged and cleared have not.

CHAPTER 11

REAL LIFE EXPERIENCES

The Cases

So far, we've covered the basic fundamentals of what constitutes a sex crime in California; and, I think it's helpful to apply that information to real-life, actual scenarios from my actual cases to better illustrate how this information may apply to you or a loved one.

In my 28 years of practicing law I've handled every type of sex crime case from casual kissing in the gym by two high school students to kidnapping and forced sexual assault.

Many times, cases arise from parties, one-night-stands, and casual dates. You know the scenario: You're with someone you don't really know; you're in an environment in which you're not familiar; alcohol and/or drugs are involved where the sources are unknown; your accuser is intoxicated. Often, you're intoxicated. You wake up the next morning wondering…what happened? Did we have sex?

Again, the law dictates that if you're sexually involved with someone who is drunk or unconscious, and it is clear that they are unable to give consent (the word "clear" is subjective) YOU are guilty of a sex crime.

Everyone needs to understand and appreciate the problems that exist when you are at a party drinking and engaged in a sexual act with someone. You are putting yourself in jeopardy with a chain-of-events that can alter your life. There could be serious questions regarding the ability of the person you share the sexual act with to have physically or verbally consented.

Absence of strong evidence of consent, you could be investigated by the police, charged by the Prosecutor, and face a trial where your life would be placed in the hands of a jury.

CHAPTER 12

FREQUENTLY ASKED QUESTIONS

- **Is Sexting a Sex Crime?**

Sexting among adults is legal in California

- **What is the Age of Consent in California?**

The age of consent in California is 18 years of age.

- **What is the Romeo & Juliet Law?**

This law typically allows someone over the age of 14 to consent to have sex with someone who is no more than three years older than them. California does NOT have a Romeo and Juliet Law.

- **Can a Minor be charged with Statutory Rape with Another Minor?**

Yes. In California Statutory Rape occurs when a person engages in sexual intercourse with someone under 18. It is usually charged when an adult has sex with a minor but can also occur between two minors.

In California, a 17-year-old could be charged with Statutory Rape for having consensual sexual intercourse with a person 17 years old or younger.

- **Is It Possible to Rape a Spouse?**

Yes. Spousal Rape is nonconsensual sex in which the perpetrator is the victim's spouse. Spousal Rape is illegal in all 50 US states.

- **What is Rape in Concert?**

In California, you can be equally charged with Rape if you knew the perpetrator's plans to commit rape, intended to help carry out the crime, and actually assist, facilitate or encourage the rape through words or actions. This is the definition of "Rape in Concert".

- **I Have a Warrant – What's Next?**

Contact a criminal defense attorney immediately.

An outstanding warrant is a serious matter and not something you should try to handle on your own. An experienced attorney will know the law and pertinent procedures and can advise you on your options.

INDEX

NOTES

Made in the USA
Monee, IL
05 November 2026

67385075R00038